Flowers And Butterflies
Large Print Easy To Read Dot-to-Dot
From 153 to 527 Dots

By Laura's Dot to Dot Therapy

Copyright © 2018

<u>How To Use This Book</u>

Hi! We're so glad you're a lover of puzzles and dot connecting- we are too!

Connecting the dots in this book is simple- just relax and follow the numbers in consecutive order, drawing a straight line between each one. Dot 1 will connect to dot 2 and so on and so forth until there are no more dots to connect. There's always another dot and you'll always find it. Connect every dot to discover the beautiful images they create.

In case you get lost or can't find a dot, never stress- there's an answer key at the back of the book that will show you exactly where each dot connects to the next. If you want to color your images, we encourage you to do so! Feel free to try all different colors and coloring mediums for your images!

If you find any errors or omissions in this book, email us at Laurasdottodot@gmail.com and please let us know! We want you to have the best dot to dot experience!

Page 1

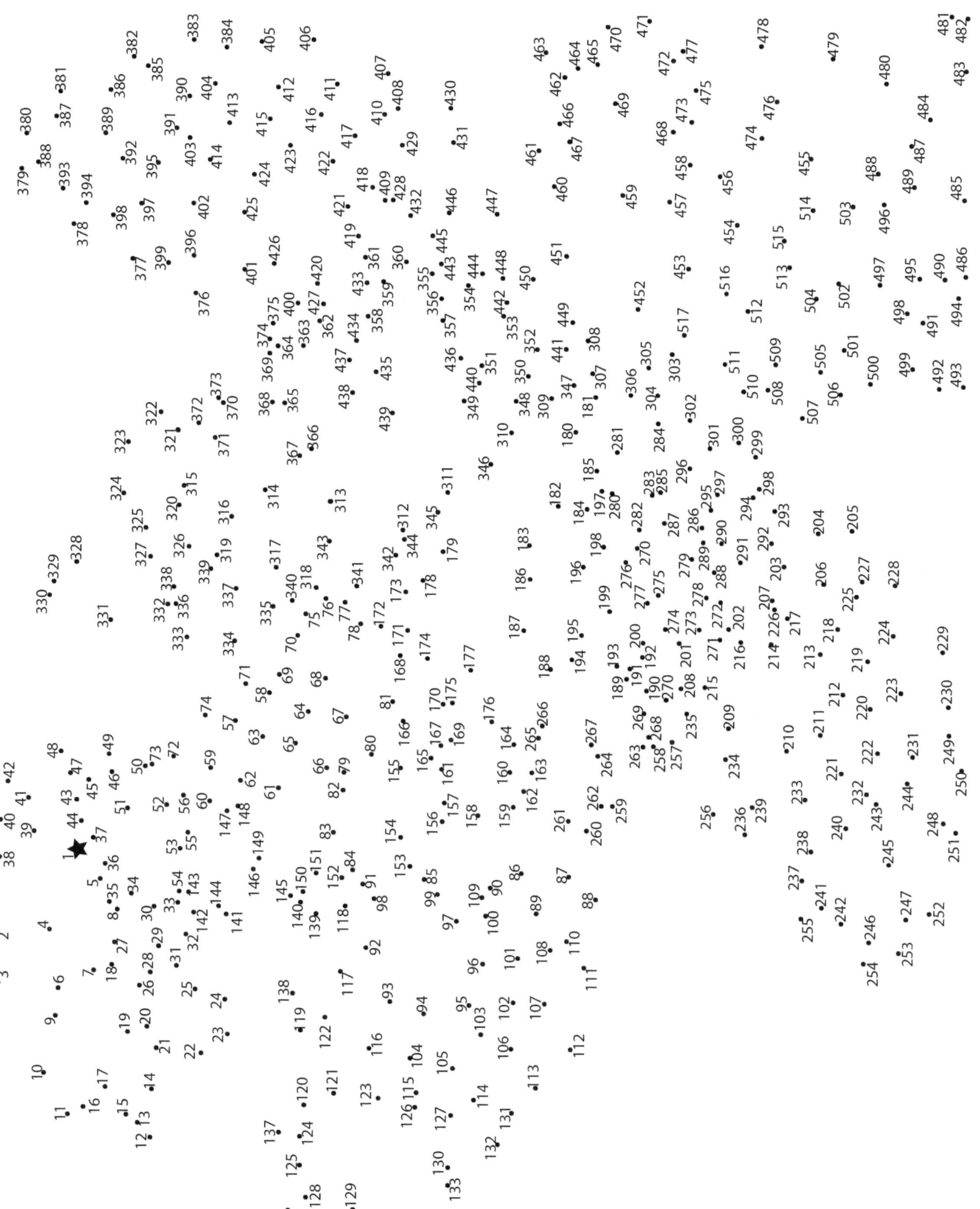

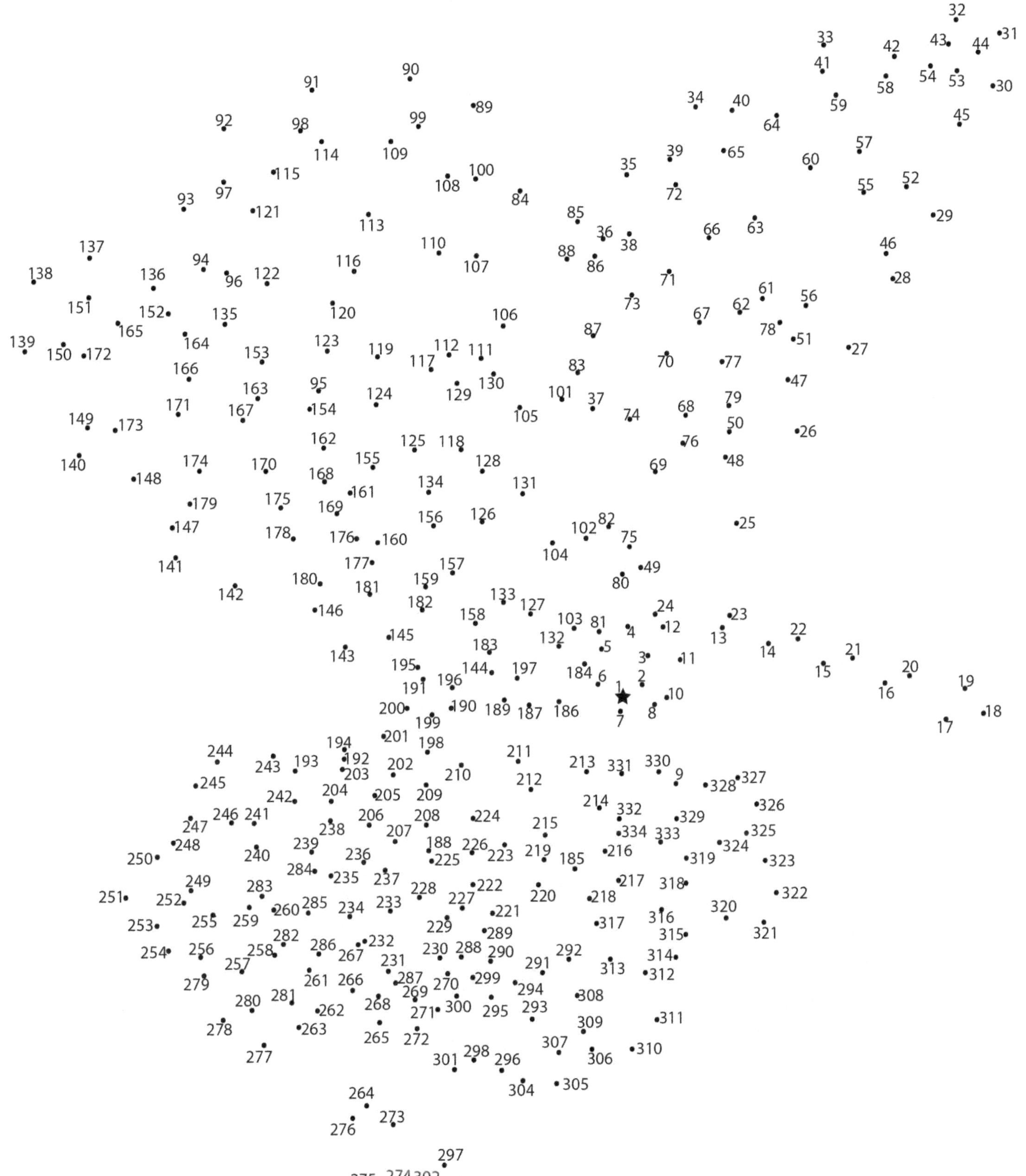

Enjoy bonus images from
some of our other fun
dot-to-dot books

Find all of our books on Amazon

Famous Movies and Movie Posters
Dot-to-Dot For Adults

Cute Baby Animals Dot-to-Dot
Puzzles from 150 to 446 Dots

409 411 412
397 396 398 399 410 408
397 392 395 400 401 407 413 421
390 387 393 394 403 402 404 405 406 416 414 422 420
388 385 386 42 41 423
384 43 40 415 417 419 424 429
389 383 376 44 39 38
382 65 54 37 418 425 430
377 375 55 53 66 64 57 56 52 45 36 426 428 431
373 67 63 58 50 46 47 48 49 35 439
378 60 51 427 432
381 62 59 34 434 438
372 68 61 33 440
379 69 10 433 437 441
374 366 70 12 11 9 32 435
380 367 365 72 71 13 4 3 2 8 31 446
370 306 5 1 30 442
359 305 307 73 14 6 7 15 436
368 364 304 308 310 75 74 16 22 24 443
360 309 328 326 76 17 23 25 29 445 447
369 358 342 303 311 18 19 20 26 27 28 444 448
363 344 343 329 312 327 325 77 78 79 80 111 112 81 113 120 122
345 357 341 301 314 316 317 318 320 322 82 83 110 114 119 121 115 123
362 353 354 340 302 313 315 91 319 90 84 109 118 126 124 127
346 352 339 334 333 332 330 89 108 116 117 128
347 351 350 299 335 331 288 287 92 95 98 88 87 86 85 107 101 102 103 104 105 106 125
348 349 337 336 298 296 293 289 93 94 96 97 99 100 129
143 297 295 294 292 290 286 136 135 134 133 132 131 130 210
142 144 141 140 139 138 137 285 257 250 249 241 240 239 231 230 221 220 211 209
145 281 282 283 284 258 242 232 229 222 219 212
280 274 273 266 265 256 251 248 238 228 223 218 213 208
146 275 272 267 264 259 243 233 214 207
147 279 276 271 268 263 260 255 252 247 237 234 227 224 217 215 206
148 278 277 270 269 262 261 254 253 246 245 236 235 226 225 216 205 163
196 197 198 199 200 201 202 181 203 204 172 162
149 195 193 189 183 179 180 176 175 174 173 171 164
150 191 192 194 187 188 182 184 177 178 167 168 169 170 165 159 160 161
151 186 185 166 158
152 153 154 155 156 157

ANSWER KEY

Follow along with the
page numbers from top left
to bottom right

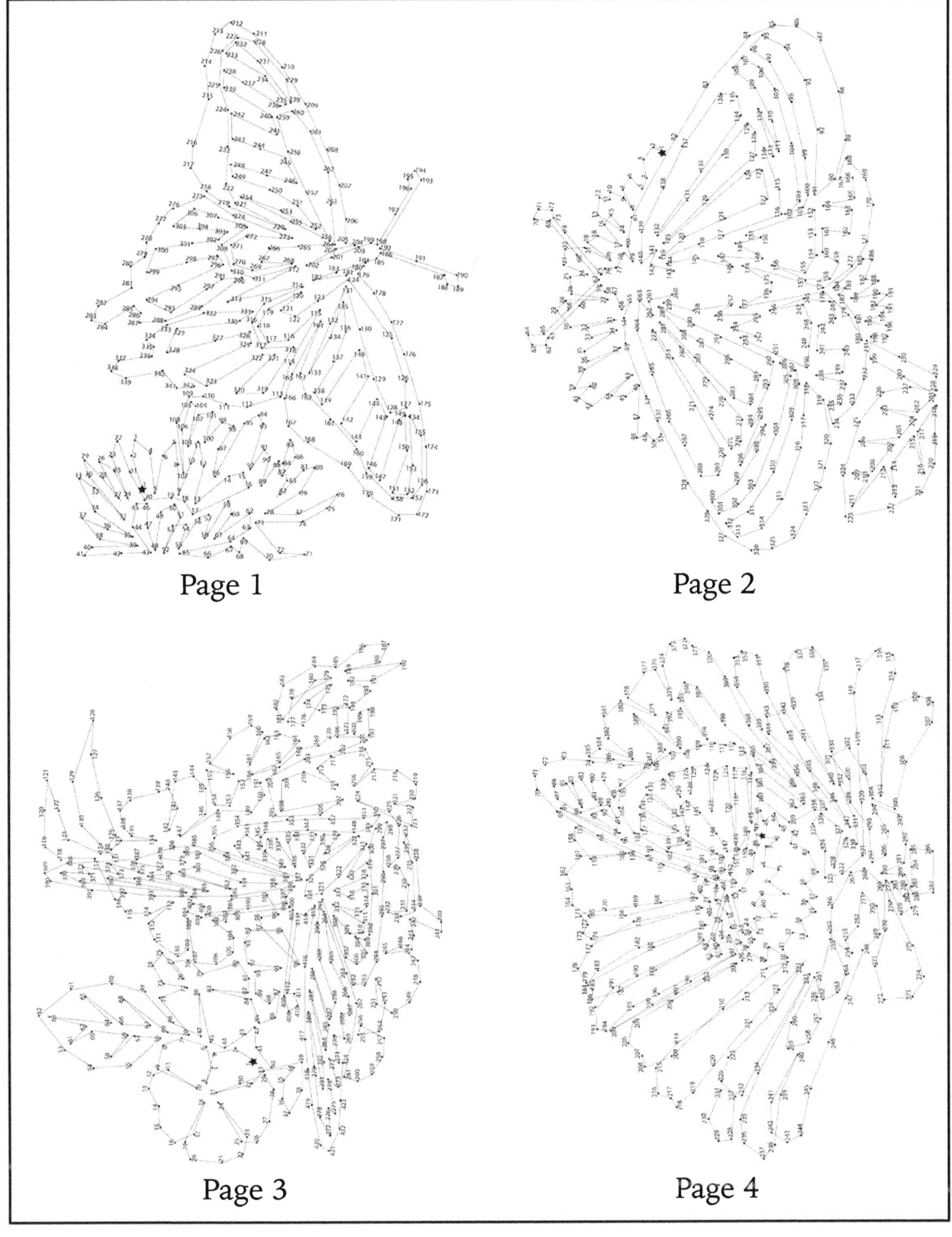

Page 1

Page 2

Page 3

Page 4

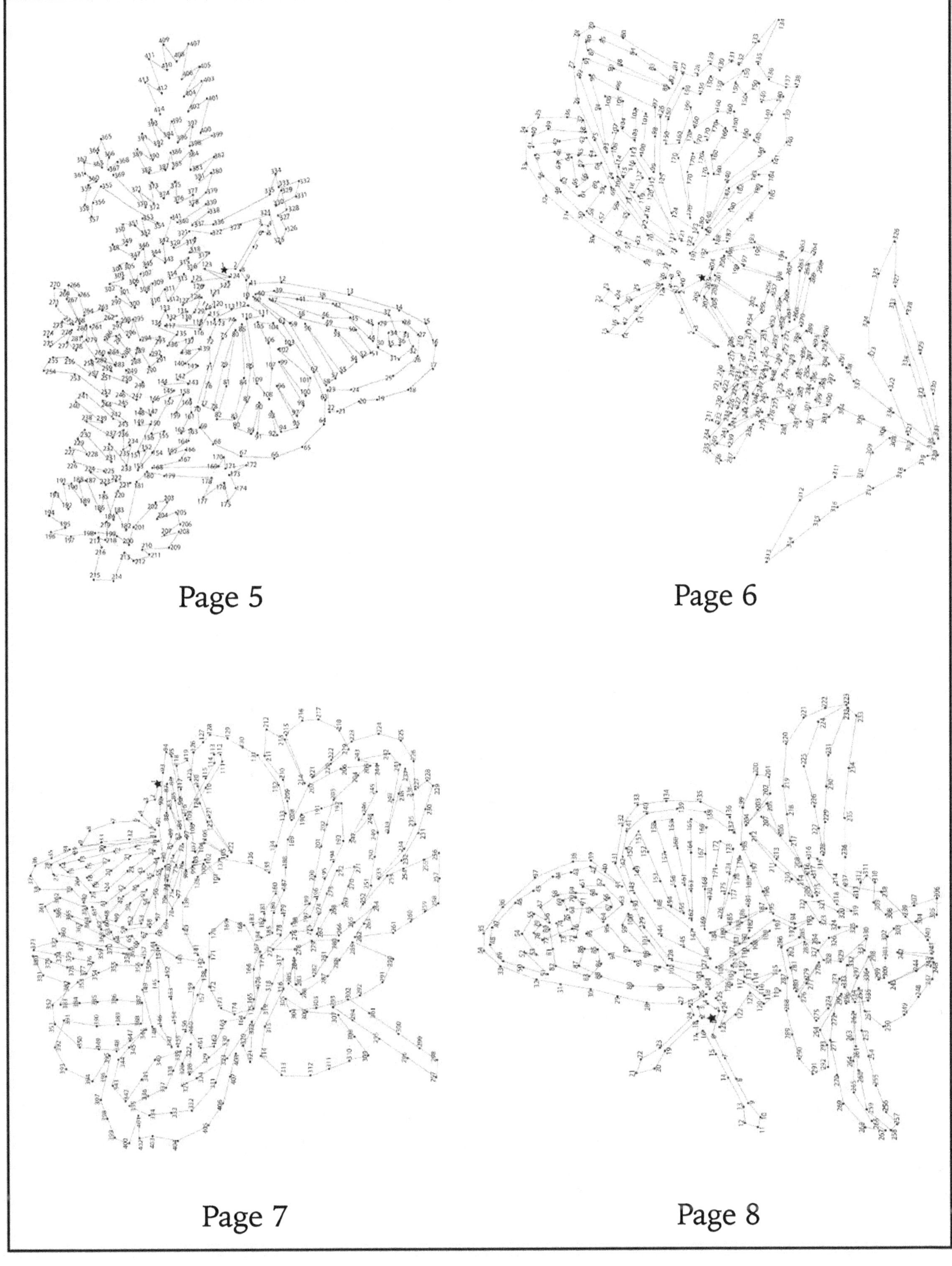

Page 5

Page 6

Page 7

Page 8

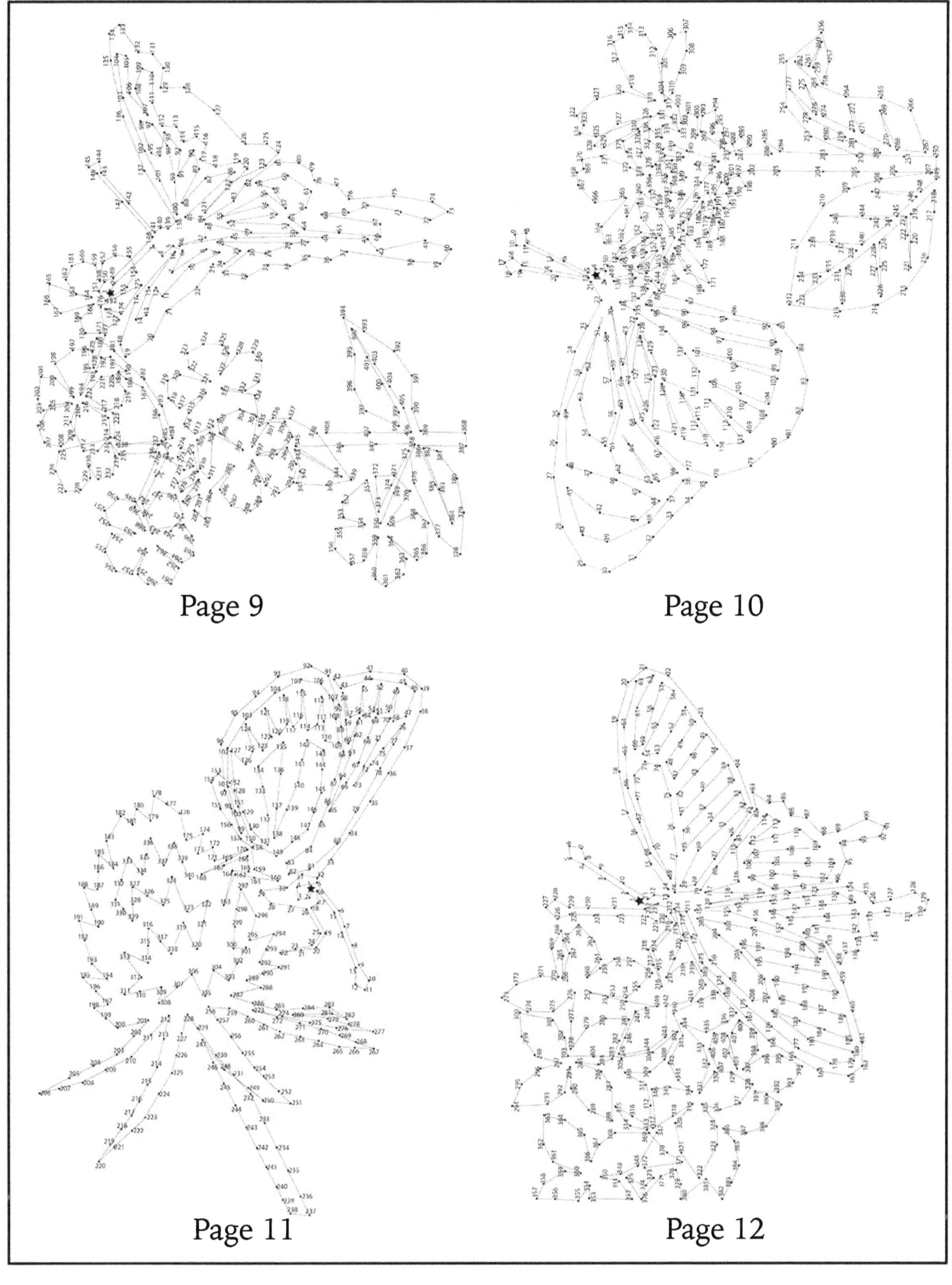

Page 9

Page 10

Page 11

Page 12

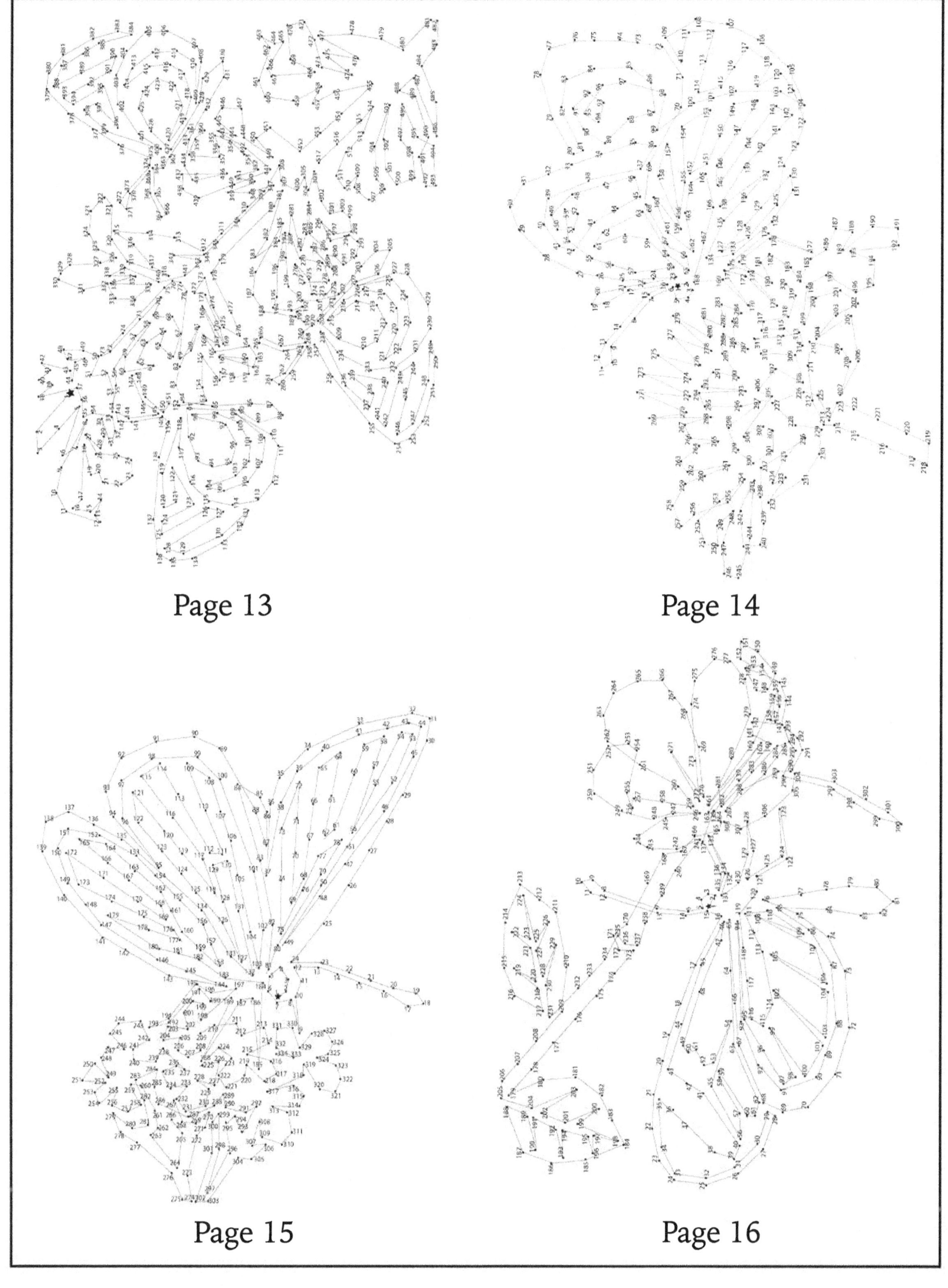

Page 13

Page 14

Page 15

Page 16

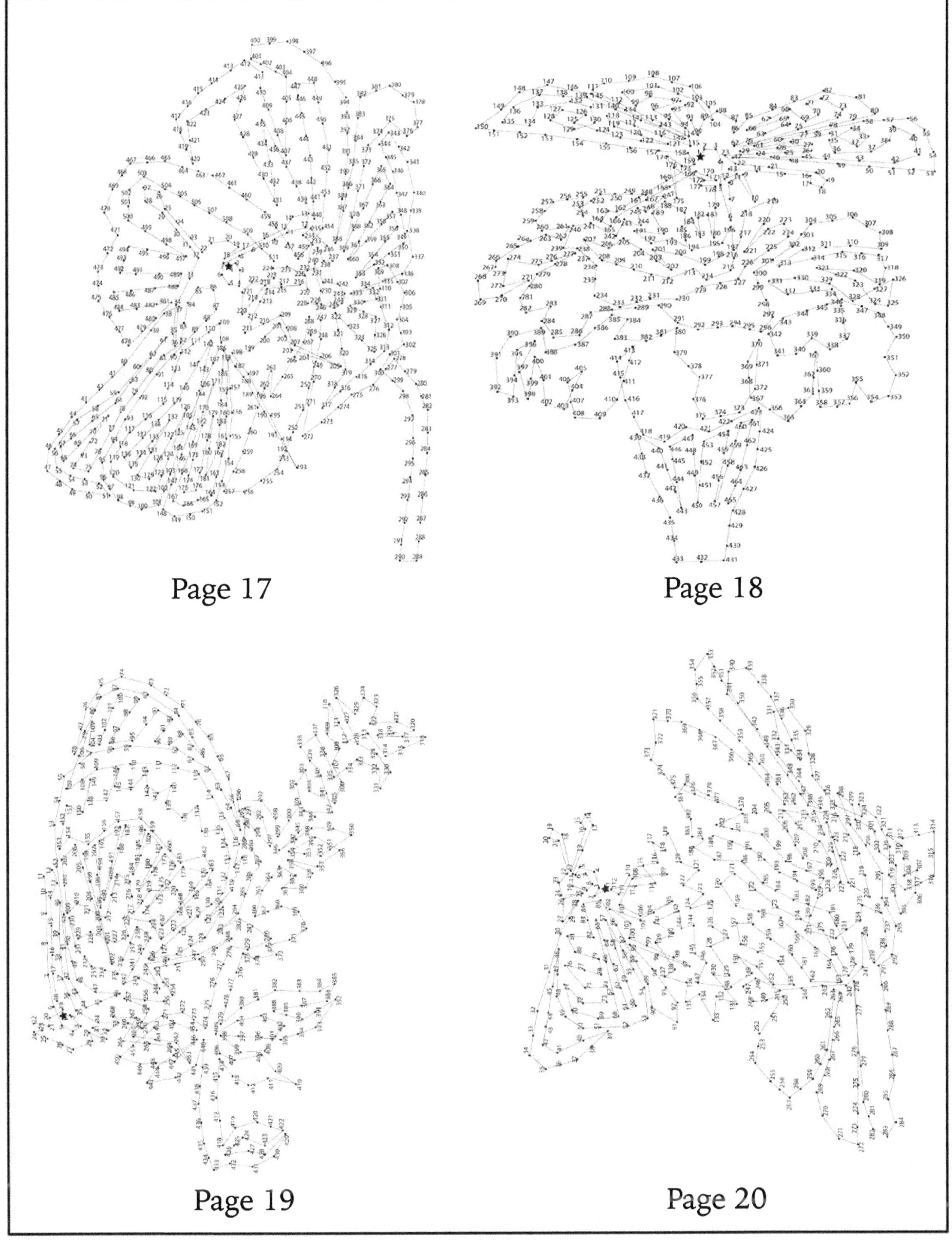

Page 17

Page 18

Page 19

Page 20

Please
Leave
Us
A Review
On Amazon

www.ingramcontent.com/pod-product-compliance
Lightning Source LLC
Chambersburg PA
CBHW081534250726
48659CB00009B/2992